Science in Ancient Mesopotamia

Carol Moss

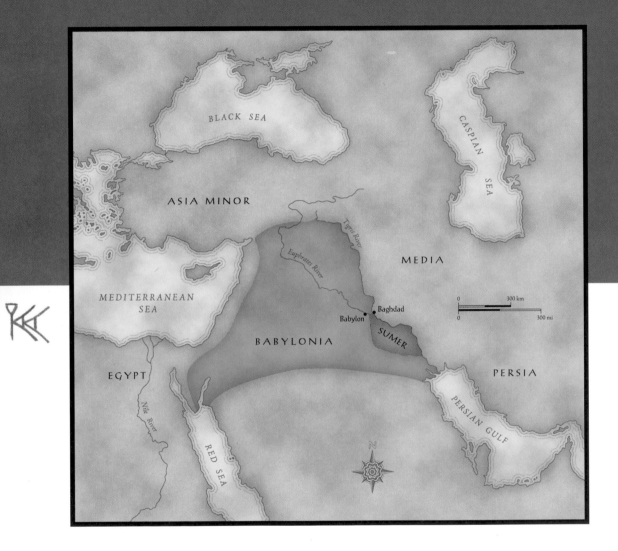

BLACK SEA

CASPIAN SEA

ASIA MINOR

MEDITERRANEAN SEA

MEDIA

Tigris River

Euphrates River

Baghdad

Babylon

SUMER

BABYLONIA

PERSIA

EGYPT

Nile River

PERSIAN GULF

RED SEA

0   300 km

0   300 mi

N

Science in Ancient Mesopotamia

Carol Moss

Science of the Past

FRANKLIN WATTS

A Division of Grolier Publishing

New York • London • Hong Kong • Sydney

Danbury, Connecticut

Photographs ©: Ancient Art & Architecture Collection: 8, 10, 24, 40, 28, 34, 49 (Ronald Sheridan); Art Resource: cover, 11, 18, 32, 43, 45, 51, 53 (Erich Lessing), 14; Bridgeman Art Library: 20, 39, 41, 52, 55, 56; ET Archive: 7, 15, 44, 47, 48, 54; Giraudon/Art Resource: 6; National Library of Medicine: 16; Photo Researchers: 17, 30, 42 (Nigel Catlin), 37 (John Sanford), 31 (Sauzereau), 12 (Frank Zullo); Scala/Art Resource: 23, 25; Science Museum/Science & Society Picture Library: 27; Tony Stone Images: 36 (James Balog), 9 (Hulton Getty), 35 (Joel Simon), 33 (Ralph Wetmore); UPI/Corbis-Bettmann: 46.

Map created by XNR Productions, Inc.

Illustrations by Drew Brook Cormack Associates

Library of Congress Cataloging-in-Publication Data

Moss, Carol (Carol Marie)

Science in ancient Mesopotamia / Carol Moss. -Rev Ed.

p. cm. — (Science of the past)

Includes bibliographical references and index.

Summary: Describes the enormous accomplishments of the Sumerians and Babylonians of ancient Mesopotamia in every scientific area, a heritage which affects our own everyday lives.

ISBN 0-531-20364-6 (lib. bdg.)   0-531-15930-2 (pbk.)

1. Science—Iraq—History—Juvenile literature.   2. Science, Ancient—Juvenile literature. 3. Iraq—Civilization—To 634—Juvenile literature.   4. Sumerians—History—Juvenile literature. [1. Science—Iraq—History.   2. Science, Ancient   3. Iraq—Civilization—To 634   4. Sumerians—History.]   I. Title.   II. Series.   I. Title.   II. Series.

Q127.I7M67   1998

509.35—dc21   97-24030
                                                           CIP
                                                           AC

Printed in China

7 8 9 10 R 10 09 08 07   62

CONTENTS

chapter 1

Ancient Mesopotamia: Where Science Began

Ancient Mesopotamians transport-
ing a load of wood up the Euphrates
River

Mesopotamia means "between the rivers." Ancient Mesopotamia was a triangle-shaped area of land located between the Tigris and Euphrates rivers. Today this land falls within the borders of three countries—Syria, Turkey, and Iraq.

People began to settle in Mesopotamia more than 8,000 years ago. They were attracted to this area because the soil was ideal for growing crops. When the rivers flooded each spring, clay and silt containing large quantities of nutrients were washed downstream and deposited in southern Mesopotamia. This is where the world's first *civilization* developed.

Mesopotamians often planted crops, such as sugar cane, along the shores of rivers or streams.

7

Even though the soil in Sumer—the country that made up southern Mesopotamia—was rich, the climate could be very harsh. Sometimes, no rain fell for 8 months. In summer, temperatures often reached 110°F (43°C) in the shade! These severe conditions encouraged the *Sumerians* to begin thinking and working together. They designed irrigation systems for their large fields of crops and built the world's first cities. They also began to explore nature and their place in it.

One of their most important early accomplishments was a system of writing. The Sumerians used clay to make writing tablets. They recorded information using a written language consisting of small wedges and lines, which they pressed into the clay tablets with tools made of bone, reed, or wood. By decoding this ancient writing, we have read their accounts of comets streaking through the night sky. Some Sumerian tablets give medical instructions, while others list mathematical formulas. Scribes also made long lists of plants and animals on tablets and clay maps of the world around them.

About 4,300 years ago, a group of people called the Akkadians conquered Sumer. The Akkadians and other Semites—groups of people who

The text on this clay tablet includes the first recorded sighting of Halley's comet.

spoke a language related to Arabic and Hebrew—ruled Mesopotamia for the next 1,800 years. They included such groups as the *Babylonians,* the Assyrians, and the Amorites.

About 2,500 years ago Mesopotamia became part of Persia. Since that time, Mesopotamia has been ruled by many groups of people. In 1921, the land that was once Sumer became part of Iraq.

Ancient Mesopotamia is often called the "cradle of civilization." It was also the birthplace of science and technology. The people living there explored the world around them and made a variety of discoveries that have shaped our own understanding of medicine, mathematics, astronomy, and chemistry. More importantly, they used what they had learned to improve their lives.

At the end of World War I, the Mespot Commission was set up to discuss the future of Mesopotamia. In 1921, the group voted to give the area that was once Sumer to Iraq.

chapter 2
Ancient Healing

A clay tablet describing healing
techniques used by ancient
Mesopotamians

y carefully deciphering their ancient clay tablets, we have learned how the Mesopotamians treated conditions ranging from mental illness to baldness.

Because these ancient people were very superstitious, they relied on two types of healers. The *asu,* or "water-knower," treated the body and gave medicines. About 4,500 years ago a Mesopotamian asu wrote the following prescription for an unknown disease:

> *Sift and knead together—all in one—turtle shell, the sprouting naga-plant, salt [and] mustard; wash [the sick part] with quality beer [and] hot water; scrub [the sick part] with [the mixture]; after scrubbing, rub with vegetable oil [and] cover with pulverized fir.*

The Mesopotamians believed that the herbal remedies prescribed by the asu could reduce a fever or slow an infection. However, they felt that the only real cure for any illness was to please the angry god who had

The middle section of this bronze plaque shows a Mesopotamian healer and a priest visiting a sick person. The priest is dressed like a fish.

sent a demon to invade the victim's body. So the second type of healer, called the *ashipu* or "conjurer," was an expert in magic.

The ashipu knew which gods demanded prayers, sacrifices, chants, and magic rituals. The two types of healers sometimes worked together, combining medicine and chants like this one found on an ancient clay tablet:

Let the evil demon leave;

let the demons strike at each other.

May the good spirit enter the body.

To understand the will of the gods, the Babylonians searched for divine meaning in daily events. Dreams, shooting stars, the birth of deformed animals, or even the flight patterns of birds might be signs from

The Babylonians believed that a shooting star was a sign from the gods.

the gods. If a healer saw a black dog or a black pig while he was on the way to a patient's home, it was a sign that the patient would die. A white pig meant that the patient would live. Healers also believed the patient would recover if a snake fell on the sick person's bed.

The Babylonians filled tablet after tablet with lists of symptoms, grouped by different organs and body parts. They believed that if a patient's brow and tongue were white, the illness would be long, but the patient would live. However, death was expected if the patient's face was white and overcast with yellow, the mouths and lips were full of ulcers, and the left eye twitched.

Studying the Body

The Mesopotamians noticed that sometimes one family member became sick just as another was getting better. They concluded that the demon responsible for the illness had moved from one person to another. To give the family peace, healers often tried to pass the demon on to animals.

They would place a lamb or a young goat near the patient and perform a special ritual. Later, they killed the animal and cut it open. If the animal had a diseased liver, lung, or any other sign of illness, the healer declared the ceremony a success. This good news may have helped some patients. Today we know that a positive attitude is an important part of many cures.

As healers looked at the intestines and organs of animals, they learned about parts of the body. People also made discoveries from butchering or sacrificing animals. To learn more about the human body, the Mesopotamians may have studied the corpses of people who died in accidents or warfare.

Physicians recorded what they learned on clay tablets. These tablets tell us that the ancient Mesopotamians believed the heart was the center of thought and knowledge. By Babylonian times, people considered blood to be the fluid of life. They were also intrigued by the largest human organ, the liver, because it is oddly shaped and full of blood. The Babylonians thought it must be the center of emotions and of life itself! They tried to predict the future by examining the livers of sheep and goats. They believed that all the lines, spots, and wrinkles had meaning.

Mesopotamian healers learned about the structure and function of the human body by studying the internal organs of sacrificed animals. This section of a huge wooden gate shows a bull and ram on their way to a sacrificial altar.

A clay model of a liver inscribed with cuneiform writing

Reading the liver was so important that the Babylonians made clay models of livers and covered them with *cuneiform* writing that described the connection between physical features and future events.

The First Drugs

Mesopotamian healers often wrote prescriptions on clay tablets. Many examples of such prescriptions have been found by archeologists. Unfortunately, it is difficult to determine what disease or ailment these medications were intended to cure. And there is very little information about the

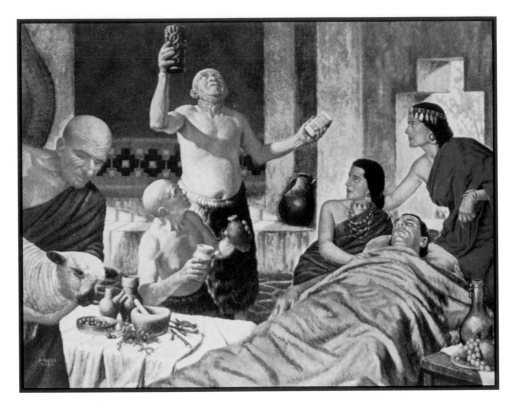

Babylonian healers made medicines from flowers, roots, leaves, nuts, snake-skins, and turtle shells.

proper dosage—the amount of medication to be taken. This may be because the ancient healers kept their remedies secret. It is also possible that the healers experimented with each patient to see which treatment worked best!

Healers made the first drugs from plant, animal, and *mineral* matter. Many remedies contained herbs, such as thyme, and the leaves, stems, and roots of shrubs and trees including myrtle, fir, cassia, and willow. Today a bitter chemical found in the bark and leaves of certain willows is an important ingredient in aspirin.

Milk, snakeskin, and turtle shell found their way into many remedies. Fruit trees such as the pear, fig, and date were also common in early drugs.

16

Healers stored seeds, roots, branches, bark, and gum in small batches. Later they ground these materials into powder and mixed them with other ingredients. They often added wine or cedar oil to make the remedies spread easily. Sometimes they mixed medications with milk or beer to hide the drugs' unpleasant taste.

Mesopotamian healers often used salt as an *antiseptic* to clean wounds. They used saltpeter, a substance used today in processed meats such as bologna and bacon, to help close wounds.

Early Surgery

If chants and prescriptions didn't help a patient, a surgeon might be necessary. Scientists have unearthed skulls that show signs of a mysterious surgical practice called *trephination.* If disease caused the brain to swell inside the skull, surgeons sometimes cut out a small piece of skull bone to relieve the pressure. Later, when the swelling decreased, they replaced the piece. Some skulls showing this kind of surgery are almost 7,000 years old.

The Babylonians were the first people to make laws about medicine. Laws set down by King Hammurabi

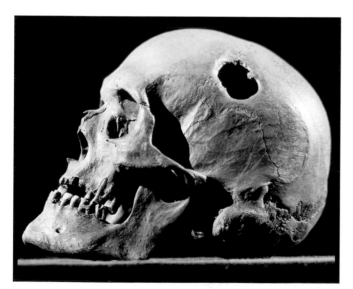

A medical procedure called trephination may have been performed on this man to reduce brain swelling.

This black basalt
carving depicts
King Hammurabi
standing before the
sun god Shamash.

required that surgeons be rewarded if they were successful—and punished if they were careless! The rewards or punishments depended on the social class of the patient. A surgeon who saved the life of a member of the nobility received 10 shekels of silver. For a common citizen, the reward was 5 shekels; for a slave, 2 shekels. But what if a surgeon made a mistake? If a surgeon failed to save a person of high rank, one hand was cut off. If the unlucky patient was a slave, the surgeon had to repay the owner the cost of the slave.

Even though most ancient medical cures relied on signs and superstition, the Mesopotamians deserve credit for many important discoveries. They were the first group of people to study the human body and how it works.

chapter 3
Developing Mathematics

A Babylonian tablet describing
mathematical theories

Early in their history, the people of ancient Mesopotamia began exploring ways to count, write numbers, and solve mathematical problems. The Sumerians worked out the basic ideas of mathematics about 3,800 years ago. No other civilization was able to match this accomplishment for another 1,500 years.

Even before the Sumerians understood basic math, ancient people used their ten fingers for counting. For that reason, the earliest arithmetic depended on a base ten, or *decimal,* number system. The Arabic system of numbers, which most of the world uses today, is a decimal system. In Mesopotamia, mathematicians invented a second number system built around a base of sixty. This more complex system is called a *sexagesimal* system.

If you look at the table on the next page, you will notice that the sexagesimal symbols seem to make sense until 60. The symbol for 60 is the same as the symbol for 1. The symbol for 70 is the equivalent of 60 + 10. Compare the symbol for 70, $\Bbbk$, to the symbol for 11, $\triangleleft$.

The symbol for 80 was $\Bbbk\!\!\!\triangleleft$, while 12 was written as $\triangleleft\!\!\!|$. The symbol for 100 was nothing special in this system, but the symbol for 120 was. It was written as $\mathbb{m}$, which could be expressed as two groups of 60. Similarly, 180 was written as $\mathbb{m}$.

Some counting and measuring tasks used the decimal number system and others used the sexagesimal system. Weights were calculated using a system based on the typical load that could be carried by a person

NUMERIC SYMBOLS

Arabic	Sexagesimal		Arabic	Sexagesimal
1			10	
2			20	
3			30	
4			40	
5			50	
6			60	
7			70	
8			80	
9			90	
			100	

A Sumerian weight in the form of a goose

or an animal. This load, called a *talent,* was divided into 60 minas, and each mina into 60 shekels. One talent weighed about 67 pounds (30 kg).

Giving Numbers Value

In the counting system we use today, the position of the number—its *place value*—is very important. To us, the 3 in 321 means three hundreds, while the 3 in 123 means three units. The Sumerians were the first people to use the idea of place value in written numerals.

Place value gave scribes an easy way to write large numbers on their tablets. Because the Sumerians used the position of a numeral to determine its value, their number system had a limited number of symbols. Those symbols could be combined to represent any number, no matter how small or how large.

In some ancient cultures, people used different symbols for a number when it had different place values. Addition and subtraction were much more difficult with the number systems used by the ancient Egyptians and Romans.

A Symbol for Zero

Imagine what a number system would be like without a symbol for zero. It's hard to believe, but for many centuries the Sumerians had no symbol for zero. When they wrote a numeral with a zero in it, they simply left a blank space. If we followed this method today, we would write the numeral 504 as 5 4. This way of indicating zero can be tricky. If a scribe copying a clay tablet did not notice the empty space, he might accidentally omit it.

About 2,300 years ago, the Babylonians came up with a solution to this problem. They invented a symbol to represent none or nothing. No other culture thought about introducing a zero symbol for another 2,000 years.

Mesopotamian scribes recording booty recovered during a battle. Later, mathematicians would calculate its value.

These clay tablets show a discussion of the properties of right triangles (left) and a square divided into two right triangles (right).

Evidence of Mathematical Knowledge

Ancient mathematicians left us many tablets that show how they worked with numbers and mathematical ideas. Some tablets have row after row of numbers and calculations, much like the numeric tables in modern math textbooks. Others are arranged like multiplication tables.

One ancient tablet shows a square with a diagonal line that divides it into two *right triangles.* Symbols pressed into the clay show calculations that compare the lengths of each triangle's sides to its *hypotenuse.* The hypotenuse is the side of the triangle opposite the right angle. This tablet was an important discovery. It shows that the Babylonians were the first people to use the formula we now call the Pythagorean theorem. The Babylonians were using this formula more than 1,000 years before the Greek philosopher Phythagoras, for whom it was named!

The Mathematics of Everyday Life

The Mesopotamians were the first people to use a number system as a basis for weights and measures. Mathematics became important for weighing everything from grain to precious metals. The creative

An Early Math Problem

Some Mesopotamian tablets listed numbers that mathematicians could insert into mathematical formulas to solve problems. Other tablets used words to describe mathematical problems and their solutions—much like the problems in modern textbooks. Here's an example:

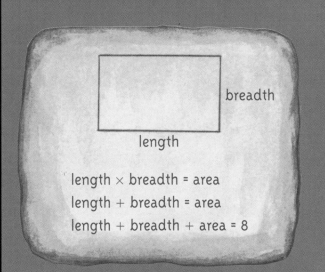

breadth

length

length × breadth = area
length + breadth = area
length + breadth + area = 8

A rectangle.* I have multiplied the length by the breadth and have thus obtained the area. I added the length and the breadth and the sum is equal to the area. I added the length, the breadth, and the area, and the total sum of all three is eight. What are the dimensions?

Can you solve this problem?

*Hint: A square is a type of rectangle.

This set of bronze
weights was used
by the Babylonians.

Mesopotamian mathematicians were also the first to use fractions.
Fractions allowed for more precise counting, weighing, and measuring
when people bought and sold goods. Some merchants used a measurement called the "grain," which was was based on the weight of a kernel
of corn.

A clay tablet that
lists the areas of a
Babylonian farmer's
fields

Measurements of length were based on the *cubit,* which was about 20 inches (51 cm) long. The Babylonian mile was more than six times greater than the modern mile, and more than ten times longer than a kilometer. Land area was measured by a unit called the "field," which was slightly smaller than 1 acre (0.4 hectare). Sometimes a plot of land was measured by the quantity of grain that could be planted in it. The Sumerians devised mathematical formulas to calculate the volume of their canals and then used this information to determine how much water to deliver to their parched fields.

The Sumerians and Babylonians invented complex formulas for calculating wages based on workdays and fractions of workdays. They decided how shares of property should be divided among family members. They even computed interest on money as it grew over months and years, just as banks do today.

The Sumerians and Babylonians were very skilled at counting, calculating, weighing, and measuring. Their knowledge influenced other cultures centuries later. They used both of their number systems to measure their observations and record their discoveries. They were ready to study events in the largest laboratory of all—the sky.

chapter 4

Exploring the Skies

The ancient Mesopotamians used the movement of the stars to measure the passage of time.

The people of ancient Mesopotamia had a good reason for watching the sky. They used the changing positions of the stars, planets, and moon to measure the passage of time. Measuring time was important for planning religious festivals and for planting and harvesting crops. Because the Mesopotamians knew when to expect the yearly floods of the Tigris and Euphrates rivers, they could take precautions to protect their crops—and their lives.

Creating a Calendar

The Sumerians designed a calendar based on the phases of the moon. Each year consisted of 12 months, and each month was about 29½ days long.

In ancient Mesopotamia, the new crescent moon marked the beginning of each month.

As a result, the Sumerian year was 354 days long—12 × 29½. Each new month began when the first sliver of crescent moon appeared. Keeping track of time with this calendar could be difficult. Bad weather or a cloudy horizon sometimes made it impossible to see the new crescent moon.

Today we know that a true year is equal to the amount of time it takes Earth to circle the

A Mesopotamian calendar

sun once—about 365 days. The Sumerian year was about 11 days too short. So, as the years passed, the Sumerian calendar could not accurately predict the flooding of the Tigris and Euphrates or when crops should be harvested. To solve this problem, the Sumerians eventually learned to add an extra month to their calendar every 3 years or so.

According to the Sumerians, sunset marked the beginning of a new day. They divided each day into twelve *double hours,* and each double hour was broken into thirty parts. These divisions, which are based on the Mesopotamian sexagesimal number system, are the basis for the hours and minutes we use to describe portions of the day. These divisions also led to the decision to divide a circle into 360 parts (12 × 30). The Mesopotamians called each of these parts an *ush*. Today we divide a circle into 360 *degrees*.

Although we think of the setting sun as marking the end of day and the beginning of night, the Sumerian day began at sunset.

A View of the Universe

The Sumerians believed that Earth was a flat disk. They thought the gods moved the sun, moon, planets, and stars through the sky, which they imagined as a large dome. Between the ground and sky was the *lil,* or atmosphere. The lil constantly moved and swirled.

For many centuries, the Babylonians used clay tablets to keep detailed records of the movements of planets and stars. They used a set of thirty stars as reference points and recorded the locations of the moon and planets with respect to these stars. About 2,400 years ago, the Babylonians began using mathematical formulas to predict how the night sky changed from month to month, and how the appearance and disappearance of stars repeated year after year.

People also watched the heavens for unusual events. They recorded *comets* as bright lights with glowing tails that traveled across the sky and *meteors* as periodic streaks of light. They noted solar *eclipses* as the

This Babylonian carving shows people worshipping Shamash, the sun god, and Sin, the moon god.

During a solar eclipse, the sun temporarily disappears as the moon moves between the sun and Earth.

moon moved between the sun and Earth. They even recorded the direction in which Earth's shadow swept across the moon's face during lunar eclipses.

Tracking an Age-old Comet

Comets move around the sun in *elliptical* orbits. Halley's comet, which is named after British astronomer Edmund Halley, orbits the sun about once every 77 years. As Halley's comet approaches the sun, viewers on

Earth can see it for several days. Astronomers and historians have known for years that this comet was seen by ancient Greeks and Romans. Their records show that they viewed it more than 2,000 years ago.

When scientists took a closer look at ancient documents and made adjustments for the different calendar systems used by ancient cultures, they found that ancient Babylonian tablets stored at the British Museum in London included information about comets that had passed Earth about 76 and 152 years before the earliest one recorded by other cultures. So the ancient Mesopotamians were probably the first group of people to observe Halley's comet.

A Babylonian tablet contains the first recorded sighting of Halley's comet, which passes Earth about once every 77 years.

Orion the Hunter is one of the brightest and best known constellations. The three stars in the center of the constellation represent his belt.

Watching the Night Sky

Night after night, the people of ancient Mesopotamia tracked the position of the moon. They watched it grow from a thin crescent to a full disk and noted how it moved among the stars. They recorded when bright stars appeared on the horizon and when they disappeared from sight. They also envisioned imaginary objects and animals outlined by stars. Today we call these figures *constellations*. Examples include the Big Dipper, Cassiopeia, Draco the Dragon, and Orion the Hunter.

The Babylonians were fascinated by the planets. Mercury, Venus, Mars, Jupiter, and Saturn were bright points of light that moved among the patterns of dimmer stars. The ancient people playfully compared the wandering planets with wild sheep and the stars with domestic sheep.

Those early observers noted that the sun, moon, and planets all travel through the sky along roughly the same path. By about 2,450 years ago, they had divided this portion of the sky into twelve segments and named each one after a nearby constellation. Today we call this path the *zodiac.*

Most of the names we use to refer to the zodiac constellations are based on Latin and Greek translations of old Babylonian names. They include Aries (the Hired Man), Taurus (the Bull of Heaven), Gemini (the Twins), Cancer (the Crab), Leo (the Lion), Virgo (the Barley Stalk), Libra

Messages from the Sky

The Babylonians believed the sky held important clues to the future. At the beginning of a new year, they made predictions based on the appearance of the sky. According to Mesopotamian tablets:

- If the sky is dark, the year will be bad.

- If the face of the sky is bright when the new moon appears and [it is greeted] with joy, the year will be good.

- If the north wind blows across the face of the sky before the new moon, the corn will grow abundantly.

This painting, which was completed in 1708, illustrates the approximate positions of the zodiac constellations first imagined by the Mesopotamians.

(the Balance), Scorpio (the Scorpion), Sagittarius (the god Pablisag), Capricorn (the Goatfish), Aquarius (the Giant), and Pisces (the Tails).

As the sun travels through the sky during the course of a year, it remains in each of the twelve segments of the zodiac for 1 month. Based on careful observation, the Babylonians could predict when each of the planets would move across each sign of the zodiac. For astrologers—people who used the sky to predict the future—the zodiac provided endless possibilities for speculation.

A piece of clay tablet depicting the
Babylonians' view of the world

For the people of ancient Mesopotamia, Earth must have held as much fascination as the skies. More than 5,000 years ago, the Sumerians began making lists of the plants, animals, rocks, and minerals they encountered. Just as modern bird-watchers record each species they see, the Sumerians patiently and persistently recorded the world around them. Keeping track of this information made nature seem more orderly and predictable. The Sumerians used the tablets the way we use reference books today.

By studying nature, the Mesopotamians learned the healing powers of certain plants. They also discovered which rocks made the best paving stones and which types of fish were most tasty.

Sometimes the ancient list-makers grouped living species in strange or surprising ways. In one case, a stone, a piece of hail, and the pit from a date were all placed in the same category.

Many of the clay tablets used by the Mesopotamians still exist today. Some of these tablets contain lists of plants, animals, and rocks.

For modern scientists, these ancient lists of plants and animals are more than curiosities. They provide important clues about how the Sumerians lived, what they ate, and the changes they faced as time passed.

The World of Plants

Scribes often grouped plants by their appearance. Each description included the plant's name and the shape, size, and color of its leaves and flowers. In some cases, plants were classified by their uses. For example, plants used to make healing ointments were all listed together. Other tablets listed plant names in a certain order, much like entries in a dictionary. On still other tablets, the plants grouped together have no obvious connection. The scribe may simply have recorded random observations.

The plants in the garden of King Merodach-Baladanthea of Babylonia were grouped by their uses or shared characteristics. Garlic, leeks, and onions were grown in one part of the garden. Herbs, such as basil and mint, were grown in another area. Seasonings such as saffron, coriander, and thyme grew

Coriander in bloom

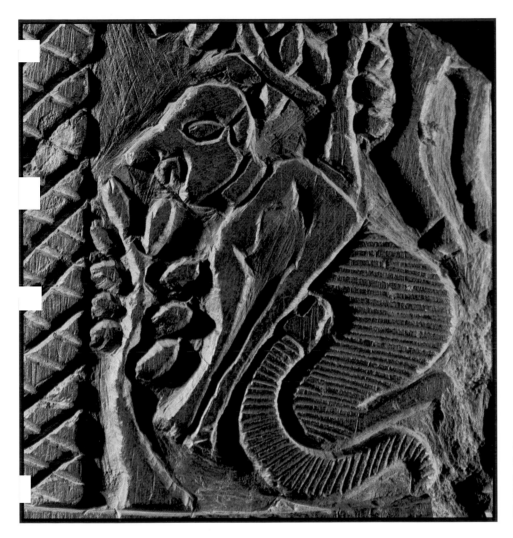

A gardener tending a small plant. A palm tree protects the small plant from the burning sun.

together. Lettuce and endive thrived side by side, as did melons and gourds. Lentils, beets, carrot-like plants, and fennel bulbs all had their places.

The garden had fruit trees, too. Date palms shared space with pomegranates. Apricot, plum, peach, and fig trees were planted together and used to shield vegetables from the scorching sun.

The animals common in ancient Mesopotamia were often depicted by artisans on vases and other containers. This ritual cup has several images of a long-bearded ram that is now extinct.

A Look at Animals

The Sumerians also made lists of fishes, snakes, birds, and other animals. Along with the designs painted on pottery, these lists tell us which animals roamed wild in ancient Mesopotamia. Mesopotamian tablets describe a number of unusual animals. There was a small horse with a camel-like head and a short, stiff mane; a humped ox that was native to India; and a graceful, long-bearded ram with curved horns.

The tablets also described animals that were important sources of food. Fish were so important that more than 100 different types were listed on Mesopotamian tablets. Among the fish commonly eaten in ancient Mesopotamia were carp, sturgeon, catfish, and eels. One list, which is about 4,000 years old, includes the names of eighteen edible fish sold at a marketplace in Larsa, a town near the Persian Gulf. These fish came from lagoons near the shore as well as from canals.

Rocks and Soil

The ancient Mesopotamians grouped rocks and minerals by appearance and by use. Some stones intrigued Sumerians because of their great beauty. Others were used to make tools, pave roads, or build houses and other structures.

An ancient Mesopotamian legend explains how rocks were named and why they had certain physical characteristics:

> One day, the god Ninurta was attacked by a group of his enemies. The rocks lying on the ground nearby began to cheer and take sides. Some believed Ninurta would win; others thought he could not overpower his enemies.
>
> Ninurta fought hard and eventually won the battle. When his enemies surrendered, he turned to the stones and began to give them names.
>
> He gave fine qualities to the loyal stones. From that time on, these rocks were prized for their beauty and usefulness. Some—such as marble and alabaster—became the best stones for statues and altars. Others—including lapis lazuli, crystalline quartz, jasper, and carnelian—became precious gems. The Mesopotamians used them to make jewelry and ornaments of worship.
>
> The hostile, disloyal stones were not so lucky. They became the common stones—the rough, dull stones used to pave streets and frame entryways. A few of the traitors became the worthless stones and pebbles that no one ever notices.

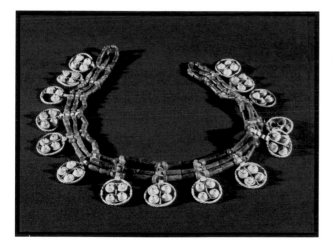

A Sumerian necklace made of gold, lapis lazuli (blue), and carnelian (red)

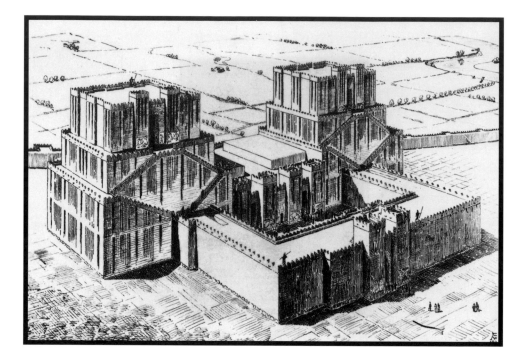

A sketch of an ancient Mesopotamian temple

When the Mesopotamians took a close look at the soil, they discovered a valuable natural resource—clay. Because it was abundant and inexpensive, clay was used to make writing tablets, pots, and jugs as well as small statues and trinkets. It was even mixed with straw and shaped into bricks to build homes and public structures. The bricks were held together with mud.

Some bricks were dried in the sun, but the Mesopotamians knew that firing them in a hot furnace made them stronger and more durable. Most pottery was also fired in furnaces. Skilled workers controlled the intensity of the fire for each specific purpose.

As the ancient Mesopotamians perfected the technology of making and baking bricks, their buildings grew taller and more impressive. The Sumerians were the first to use their engineering skills to build arches and domes, but they never mastered the art of building straight, narrow towers. Instead, they built story upon story, each level slightly smaller than the one below it.

Studying the soil also gave the Mesopotamians an opportunity to learn about sand and other *silicate* materials. Craftspeople found that when they mixed silicates with some other substances, they could create colorful glazes for their pottery. They even made fake "gems" by painting quartz pebbles with blue and green minerals that produced a solid glaze after firing. As the Mesopotamians continued to experiment with silicates, they learned to make a new material—glass.

The Sumerians also discovered that metal *ores*—including copper, gold, and silver—could be hammered and stretched into different shapes. Like bricks, pottery, and glass, the ores were strengthened by firing.

By about 4,000 years ago, the Mesopotamians had learned that they could combine copper and tin to make a stronger material called *bronze.* They used bronze to make a wide variety of objects—spears, swords, shields, knives, chisels, ax blades, pins, cups, vases, and large headdresses.

Mesopotamian soldiers used bronze shields like this one in battle more than 2,300 years ago.

This stone relief shows ancient Mesopotamian women cooking (top left), making wine (top right), butchering an animal (bottom left), and smelting metals (bottom right).

The Beginning of Chemistry

As the Mesopotamians learned about nature, they discovered ways to use natural materials to make useful products, such as drugs, soaps, and dyes. This was the beginning of chemistry. Many of the earliest chemists were women, and most of their equipment was invented in ancient kitchens. These women understood the chemical properties of food and guarded the secret formulas for the perfumes used in medicines and cosmetics as well as those for rituals and magic.

They stored, mixed, and heated substances in containers made of clay, stone, wood, or metal. Some pots had round bottoms that could be supported on rings. They looked very similar to the test tubes, flasks, and beakers used in laboratories today. Mesopotamian chemists used wool or hair to filter mixtures, so that the final product would be pure.

The chemists invented ways to make wine from figs, dates, and raisins. Sometimes they added honey or scented the mixtures with sweet-smelling perfumes or spices. They also made beer by soaking, crushing, mixing, fermenting, or sweetening barley in various ways. Ancient tablets call beer the drink that "makes the liver happy and fills the heart with joy." (Actually, alcohol is bad for the liver.) The world's oldest recipe, written on a tablet about 3,750 years ago, is a recipe for beer.

Ancient Mesopotamia had a thriving wool industry 6,000 years ago. People also realized the value of cotton, which they called "tree wool." Their amazing knowledge of chemistry allowed them to develop colorful dyes for fabrics.

A Mesopotamian woman spinning wool around a spindle

Plants Used to Make Dyes

COLOR	PLANT
Black-green	Cassia bark (a plant in the pea family)
Blue	Indigo plant
Yellow	Dried crocus flowers; turmeric (a spice)
Red	Dried insects
Purple	Mussels; lichen

The Mesopotamians discovered how to use the oils that came from sheep, birds, fish, nuts, and seeds. The Sumerians made the first soap from vegetable oils 5,000 years ago. They combined oil with wool and resin to seal the hulls of ships. They also used oil to light lamps and torches, to prepare corpses for burial, and to make medicines. Wax was useful too. Wax collected from beehives was used to protect the surface of copper objects. Carpenters used wax to preserve and finish wood surfaces.

The ancient Mesopotamians salted fish and meat to preserve it. They made glue by boiling bones, hide, and hooves into a hard mass of gelatin, and then adding water.

The Mesopotamians also preserved animal skins with tannin, which came from gall nuts, tree bark, and pomegranate rinds. They soaked the skins and rubbed them with fats and oils until they were soft and flexible. This was the first leather. The finished leather was used for harnesses and sandals, or to make pouches for drinking water, milk, or butter. The people of ancient Mesopotamia were very clever inventors. They even used inflated animal skins as "floats" to help swimmers cross rivers!

The ancienct
Mesopotamians
recorded their
process for tanning
leather.

chapter 6

The Legacy of Ancient Mesopotamia

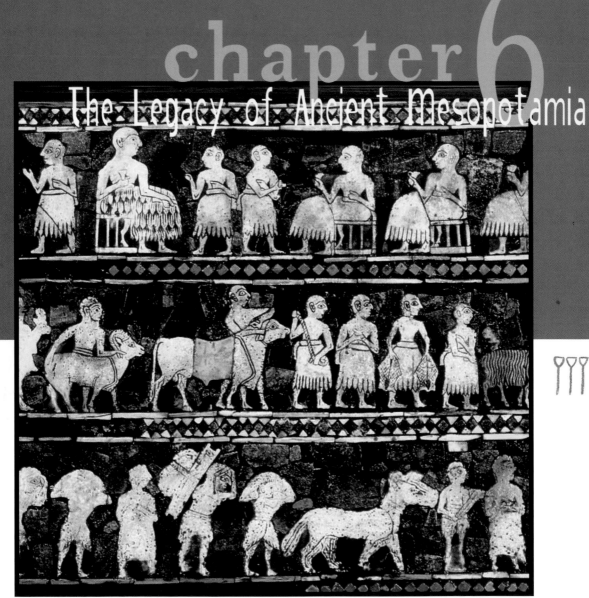

Section of a Mesopotamian mosaic

We owe a great debt to the people of ancient Mesopotamia. They were the first to study the human body and to experiment with remedies for a variety of illnesses and injuries.

In astronomy, careful record keeping is the Mesopotamians' greatest contribution. Their tablets include information that is several thousand years older than that of other ancient cultures. Whenever you see a familiar constellation, you are looking at a pattern of stars that was named by the Babylonians.

This Mesopotamian tablet contains information about the ancient view of the universe.

The Sumerians and Babylonians put mathematics to work centuries before other cultures. We still use parts of their complex number system today. We divide our day into hours, minutes, and seconds. Our use of fractions also originated in ancient Mesopotamia. The Mesopotamians were the first to use weights and measures based on a number system; and the Babylonians developed complex formulas for solving mathematical problems. Place values and a written symbol for zero are among the brilliant ideas we take for granted today.

The Sumerians also left us the first lists and simple classifications of plants and animals. These lists are very similar to the modern field guides we use to study nature.

The people of Mesopotamia invented the wheel more than 6,000 years ago. They made plows, chariots, musical instruments, and bricks. The world's oldest pottery comes from ancient Mesopotamia, land of the first potter's wheel. They also may have been the first people to build large irrigation systems.

The people of this ancient land shaped our knowledge of

This terra-cotta model of a Mesopotamian chariot or cart is about 5,000 years old.

The ancient Mesopotamians played instruments like this 4,500-year-old lyre.

Archeologists working in the Middle East have unearthed hundreds of thousands of clay tablets left behind by the ancient Mesopotamians. Many record scientific observations.

medicine, mathematics, astronomy, and earth science. Their clay tablets allow us to reach far back in time to learn how science began. Although the mysterious writing on many of these tablets has been translated, others remain stored in museums, waiting for scientists of the future. We can only imagine what secrets they may reveal.

GLOSSARY

antiseptic—a substance or process that prevents or slows down the growth of germs.

ashipu—a Mesopotamian healer who dealt with gods and demons and offered prayers, chants, or rituals as a treatment for illnesses.

asu—a Mesopotamian physician who treated the body and supplied patients with herbal remedies.

Babylonians—the people and culture that flourished in ancient Mesopotamia beginning about 3,800 years ago.

bronze—a yellowish-brown metal made by combining copper and tin.

civilization—a community of people with a relatively high level of cutural development.

comet—a small ball of ice and rock that moves around the sun in an elliptical orbit.

constellation—a group of stars in a specific area of the sky. A constellation's name comes from the imaginary object or living thing that the star pattern resembles.

cubit—an ancient measure of length usually based on the length of the forearm from the elbow to the tip of the middle finger. The Babylonian cubit was about 20 inches (51 cm) long.

cuneiform—the system of writing developed in ancient Mesopotamia. It was based on wedge-shaped characters and usually inscribed on clay tablets.

decimal—a base ten number system. The number system we use today for counting and computation is a decimal system.

degree (of a circle)—a subunit of a circle. A circle can be divided into 360 degrees. See *ush*.

double hour—a measure of time used by the ancient Mesopotamians. It is approximately twice as long as our 60-minute hour.

eclipse—a phenomenon that occurs when an object is blocked by something else. During a solar eclipse, the moon passes between the sun and Earth. As a result, the sun cannot be seen for several minutes. During a lunar eclipse, Earth casts a shadow on the moon while Earth is between the moon and the sun.

elliptical—oblong, egg-shaped. While the elliptical orbits of planets are nearly circular, the orbits of comets are extremely long and narrow. Their shape resembles a cigar.

hypotenuse—the long, diagonal side of a right triangle. The hypotenuse is always directly opposite the right angle.

lil—the swirling, expanding material that the Sumerians believed lay between Earth's surface and the dome of the heavens.

meteor—the glowing streak of light seen in the night sky when a particle of dust or rock enters Earth's atmosphere.

mineral—a non-living, naturally occurring substance with a specific chemical composition and a crystalline structure.

ore—a mineral that is mined because it contains a useful material, such as a metal or coal.

place value—the value given to the location of a digit in a numeral. In 34, for example, the location of the digit 3 has a place value of ten. The digit itself indicates three tens.

right triangle—a triangle with one 90-degree angle. Two of the sides of every right triangle are perpendicular.

sexagesimal—a system of counting and mathematical computation based on the number 60.

silicate—a mineral whose structure is composed largely of silicon and oxygen atoms; also, rocks composed of these minerals.

Sumerian—a member of the group of people that first built the civilization of ancient Mesopotamia about 5,500 years ago.

talent—a measurement of weight used in ancient Mesopotamia.

trephination—a surgical practice that called for cutting out a small piece of the skull to relieve pressure caused by swelling of the brain. When the swelling subsided, the piece of bone was replaced.

ush—a measurement based on dividing a circle into 360 parts. Today we call each of these divisions a "degree."

zodiac—the band of constellations through which the sun, moon, and planets move.

RESOURCES

Books

Aveni, Anthony. *Conversing with the Planets.* New York: Times Books, 1992.

_____. *Empires of Time.* New York: Basic Books, 1989.

Crawford, Harriet. *Sumer and the Sumerians.* Cambridge: Cambridge University Press, 1991.

Heyerdahl, Thor. *The Tigris Expedition: In Search of Our Beginnings.* New York: Doubleday, 1981.

Kramer, Samuel Noah. *History Begins at Sumer.* Philadelphia: University of Pennsylvania Press, 1981.

Krupp, Edwin. *Echoes of the Ancient Skies.* New York: Harper and Row, 1983.

Lloyd, Seton. *The Archaeology of Mesopotamia.* London: Thames and Hudson, 1984.

_____. *Foundations in the Dust: The Story of Mesopotamian Exploration.* London: Thames and Hudson, 1980.

_____. *The Ruined Cities of Iraq.* Chicago: Ares, 1980.

Thurston, Hugh. *Early Astronomy.* New York: Springer-Verlag, 1994.

Internet Sites

Due to the changeable nature of the Internet, sites appear and disappear very quickly. The following resources offered useful information on ancient civilizations at the time of publication.

Exploring Ancient World Culture includes maps, timelines, essays, and images that describe ancient civilizations in India, China, Greece, and the Near East. It can be reached at **http://eawc.evansville.edu/index.htm**

The Oriental Institute Research Archives has a site with a variety of information about ancient Mesopotamia. The address of this home page is **http://www-oi.uchicago.edu/oi/dept/ra/abzu/abzu_regindx_ meso.html**

Guide to Ancient Near East Astronomy provides information about Mesopotamian methods for viewing the night sky and recording of their observations. The home page can be reached at **http://ccwf.cc.utexas.edu/ ~hope/aneastro.html**

INDEX

ABOUT THE AUTHOR

Carol Moss received B.A. and M.S. degrees in geology from the University of Minnesota. She has been writing articles about science and technology for twenty years. She lives with her family in St. Paul, Minnesota.